The Attitudes

The Attitudes

Katie Griffiths

Nine
Arches
Press

The Attitudes
Katie Griffiths

ISBN: 978-1913437114
eISBN: 978-1913437121

First published April 2021 by:

Nine Arches Press
Unit 14, Sir Frank Whittle Business Centre,
Great Central Way, Rugby.
CV21 3XH
United Kingdom

www.ninearchespress.com

Nine Arches Press is supported using public funding by Arts Council England.

Supported using public funding by
ARTS COUNCIL
ENGLAND

Contents

I am afraid to own a Body —
– Emily Dickinson

Soul…is always in front of a mirror
– Thomas Moore

This is the light of the mind, cold and planetary.
– Sylvia Plath

And in our idleness we compare hands

He says, exorcism
improves flexibility of the hands.
Hands clarify,
throw light.

    I say, but hands are heavy-duty.
    They drag their body behind.
    And did he know, first cousin to a hand
    is not a foot but a rake. (Let the earth prepare.)

He says, to focus the disintegrating mind
you must place two fingers
on the person's eyes
before you raise the eyelids.

    I say, my fingers
    are too stiff
    from questions.

He says, it's a spiritual emergency.
He keeps a collection of items his clients
have spat out. Keys. Nails.

    I say, I keep
    a magnifying glass to study
    my hands, their wrinkling –
    a new ordinance of skin.

He says he saw four strapping men
struggle to hold down a young girl.

    I say, I held my father close
    those last minutes before his hands
    dropped like starfish
    learning the ocean.

Dough must not not enter the body

i.

One summer
she learned how to eat.

Not to swallow, just spit – crouch
with jam pastries and a paper bag.

She ate herself down to the cellar,
each night painted a portrait

of a harlot with lopsided hat
that grew with each mistake:

one botched eye had to go,
hidden by an extended brim.

Daytimes, balled against ribs
of a wooden rowboat, she'd drift

with the current, invisible
to shore, trying to occupy

less space yet at the same time
disturb it more. For wasn't that

the communion wafer's trick
on the tongues of the pious?

To dissolve. Disappear.
Do the holy work.

The Attitudes

Insipid are the moonbathers
for their light spills in small places.

Torrid are those who amass
for their trinkets will devour.

Vapid are the earthmongers
for their deals trample the nestfallen.

Rigid are those who embellish
for their fables will encrust.

Sordid are the soulscammers
for their workday sees no dusk.

Candid are those who lactate
for their largesse is passed on.

Rapid are the waterstabbers
for their targets leach away.

Sacred are those who clamber
for their vertigo instructs.

Intrepid are the scargazers
whose bodies weep for an end.

Moonbather

She is slink and fall.
A trespass in the orchard
that wrongfoots the trees.

Her darkness is famished.
She needs the kind of moon you
grind in your teeth

the kind of moon that never consoles.
How she wants to feel sorry for
you feeling sorry for her

and all the light you fail to exchange.
Under sombre whims
her reason is permeable.

See how readily she strips down
and becomes moonlogged –
innermost and full of retraction.

She wants the kind of moon
that saturates,
the kind that rains calamitous pieces.

Will you try to save her? Of course.
You'll drop footholds and rungs.
You'll call from your sill:

sister sister shake out your limbs.

Divine non-intervention

It sours your day.
Leaves a bad smell in the stairwell.
What supreme being? Unless still
lounging on Mount Olympus,

dysfunctional. Certainly mauled by all sides.
Pulled apart like moth wings.
Expanding to the required diameter.
Or none at all.

Each time you reach for the remote
you're trapped alive. To be frank,
the headlines alarm. It seems
the almighty's doing improv now.

Mother of god, you say,
lighting a candle when clearly
the only remaining option
is to address a responsible adult.

Mother of god. What on earth
were you thinking?
Carrying him
until he emptied you?

Eternal Life: The Case for Plastic

I'd argue the vindication lies in the samples of plastic:
Exhibit 3, this vial of ethanol used on Henry VIII's flagship
Mary Rose when hauled from the Solent and soaked
constantly to prevent sudden drying of ancient wood.
By extension, the testimony against Ellen Frühling,
socialite aged 74, who maintains she's had *no work done,*
despite shored-up cheeks and absence of crow's feet
that suggest the intervention of Exhibit 8b, hyaluronic acid,
injected subcutaneously by a skilful aesthetician. May I

further draw attention to this colour photograph (Exhibit 15)
of a large red amaryllis, moulded from extruded thermoplastic
and standing guard over a just visible, though tiny, mound
in a Spanish mountain cemetery. Notice the flower's mouth
peeled back to tonsils and crimson voice box, its tongues
taut from naming Teresa Rodrigo Reyes, who both arrived
and departed on February 10th 1963 at exactly 11.30am.
I contend: here's one in the eye for so-called 'death'. Blooming
in August-hard earth. Leaking no stench. Rebuffing all insects.

Minor chords – their place in the pecking order

Because she's coastal, her hair's never been cut.
She drapes it over a harp and watches
white-fronted geese on the Wexford Sloblands
draw to hunger. To pull this tight, as highly strung,
and close to the long wood, is her act of escalation.

She can't remember his name,
but his vinyl record of Breton songs drivelled
in patchy sun. Music was pliable – the hum-thrumming
for hours in her head, a version of padding in fields
that would blight then flood. Every *tap-tap* in the new-spaded
plot of the cottage in arrears tangled sound into her hair,
a coiling waterfall.
(See if a reel will not scare her toes.)
(See if a lullaby will not bludgeon her tears.)

As if she could simply march to the estuary
and drown her tunes:
Suite for Four Hands.
Prelude for Six Hands and an Elbow.
Introit for Eight Hands and a Time-Keeper.
Intercession for Ten Hands and a Big Stick.

These days, minor chords tinkle through culverts.
Smear the pavement.
Break out all over the suburbs.

She's always been soaked to the stave.

Tidal girl:
how your bed-wetting lets you down!

God's view of smoking

can only be of dragons scorching the earth,
laying bush fires, torching the crops.

God knows we are tinderbox, we are flint –
but made in his image, for clearly he's taken a drag

or two in secret. Church portraits confirm the crimp
of his lips. Whatever he's sucked in by the lungful

is neither secondary, nor passive. *Breathe on me, breath of…*
His respiratory tract ignites. Though he may have sent

his only begotten proxy to the tobacco counter, for filter-tips,
it was God himself, I'd swear, busy under the stairs,

rootling amongst my grandmother's things:
her wedding-day plait brown and dead in his hand,

and her violin, sidelined by ghostly dance,
and the instrument's black case (for all you'd think

the coffin of a missing child) sixty-five years locked
and off-limits, yet still reeking of cigarette smoke,

and his nose squashed against it,
as if smelling her for the very first time.

Nine sort-of truths*

The (*something-or-other*) of neglect forgets how it started.
Most streets eventually run themselves over.
'The emerging poet cannot escape such canonical influences'
    except by emptying a bullet-chamber, or blasting a pigeonnier.
Uncharity begins at home.
Nothing is more cleansing than a meteor shower.
Weaning is the second sign of love.
A pilgrimage done assumes the new one to begin.
All mirrors are ageist.
When the river inside you breaks its banks, you will flail and flail
    as if the water has arms you can carve into.

Nine sort-of truths* is an attempt at a **unitet, favourite of Mariana Nesbitt** who describes the form as "the fundamental opposition of cloudburst to roof ridge". Made up of disparate statements acting alone "with no coercion", the unitet provides a turn between each line, a constant *mind-the-gap*, an unexpected *Götterdämmerung*. It sets out to create in readers a sense of pitching seawards reminiscent of waiting to cross the Carrick-a-Rede Bridge – not so high, but chasmic nonetheless. The unitet's form is perfectly suited to discomfort in discovery, "no matter if the reader is irretrievably lost between lines, missing, presumed dead. Wait seven years," advises Nesbitt. "Then claim the insurance."

Mariana (just one n) Nesbitt was named after the Mariana Trench by her mother Eve O'Brien who all her life needed to dig deep. Never made it as far as Portaferry let alone the Pacific. Landlady of the Rising Sun redubbed the Rising Sin* because of the tendency of its patrons to both bed- and faith-hop at the drop of a pint, Catholic to Protestant, Protestant to Catholic, would you ever keep up? Giddy and dizzying, *she of the fancy furbelows*, it is said Eve often slept far below her station, gave birth to Mariana on a whim and a butcher's block.

***sin – actually, in its original Greek form means to 'miss the mark', 'fall short', maybe fall in a gap? An unexpected *Götterdämmerung* – did we already mention the **unitet,** perfectly suited to discomfort in any

#PowerToPardonMyself
(singing singing singing)

The priest's daily haul is no more
than the loot of a provocateur.

Lord, I've not been to the gym
or done my tummy crunch.

When I think to open my mouth
the air grows squeamish.

Nor have I marched on parliament
with a toddler in tow.

To prise words from a gullet
is to sanction a dawn raid.

Neither have I done a runner with my
things in a regulation cabin bag.

You think confessions disperse?
No, they hang about. Goading each other.

But I once made his eyes go black.

And how do you avert your glare
when a filthy soul displays itself?

Black as a sump.

J'accuse I could begin.
Correction. *Je m'accuse.*

I made his eyes go black.

Better to throw hands up,
hold oneself at knifepoint

I never knew that eyes could die.

Denunciation?
It leaves you hoarse.

you are bible and not much thumbed

'It takes nothing away from a woman of 50 years
that I don't want to sleep with her.' – Yann Moix, aged 50.

it's not that you disgust him
any page can wrinkle or bore
any curved spine points to the bookbinder's flaw

he just prefers the body of a younger woman
(whose you want to know)
(po-face preferable)

the body of a 25-year-old is extraordinary
crying out for devotion   you recollect novice monks
their ink-bites gold in your neck

the body of a 50-year-old is not extraordinary at all
with its encumbrances   and for encumbrances
read 'your decade-glass figure'

he is not responsible for his penchant
nor for wild oats nor anything pastoral
nor dog-collared men who bang on

funny isn't it
how it's your body he crushes his palm against
to swear this truth

that when he is 60
he might be able to love a woman of 50
or maybe 41   definitely 33

suck it up

you are bible
and bone loss
an embarrassing ruckus

Scargazer

(I keep saying) she must tell a different story.

Once upon a time, she says, Scar was a slow transfixing.
Scar scattered trails, openings.

Scanty Scar.
Skilful Scar.
Scary Scar.

Scar stood out
from Bootlicking Bruise and Subordinate Scratch,
who impersonated each other.

Scar – her strong arm.
Her mullion in the window.

Scar, she says, was the breakthrough,
suave as a flick,
clean as a plunge.

Come close, she says, see how easily
my arms went Scar
my back got Scar
my legs turned Scar.

I can't live with or without Scar.

Each time she tells this story
(I keep asking) aren't Scar's dues paid,
each penny a capitulation?

No, no, no – she says.
Can't you see
the grace of Scar?
Running a crack
through the urn
that wants your name.

In these weeks after you have died

each nightfall, with pencils and twigs,
I lay a trap for god.

Surely it is simple to bait him.

But the wait is long
like a discussion I have deferred.

Overhead, stars are iffy –
the sky's closed doors.

I lie low as if the grass
is a rug about to be pulled

as if the only sound worth cowering to
is the snap of a body exactly as it steps
outwitted into mid-air.

I want the twigs to break
under the weight of blunder

to deliver into my hands
the startled prey
waiting to be skinned.

Each stanza of this poem was put through
numerous versions of Google Translate

After the week of death

with pencils and shoots
I leave the skirt for god.

It's very easy to die.

Focusing on my hands
is waiting for waiting.

Above,
the stars are thereafter.

I sleep as a drop of grass, in the same
voice as the one on the left side of my body

as if the only sound worth wearing
is like a leaf
while steps are totted in the air.

I want branches to interrupt
the weight of errors

to stretch hands to the victim
looking for cover. But if you are in the air,
I'll commit a crime.

Google Translate, leave all the poems

The Priest and I Watch the Solar Eclipse Through the Safety of a Kitchen Colander

Our backs to the window, I sieve daylight
        across a piece of paper. Tricked by the pattern

of a hundred tiny suns, he is unaware that rules
        will soon be broken, has never seen a child

interrupt a sprinkler or a catamaran swerve
        in front of a ferry, flouting shipping lanes.

That the moon should be so dissident
        to make a beeline into another's orbit and hog the limelight

is an effrontery he wants to ignore. But the sun winces.
        The sky behind us falters.

The bright circles on the page are overcome. I give him
        the colander to hold. He scoops his hand inside

as though it is a tadpole net whose dark wriggling catch
        must, like salt, be thrown over his shoulder.

Purgatory

Wriggling souls
are migratory
hoping the state
is transitory
like being lost
in a multi-storey
or confined
to a dormitory
where all's forbidden
not participatory
no chance to be
exploratory.
Whether they finesse
it into allegory
the clamour to leave
grows to a furore
heard ever more:
that old sob story.

Door, my tribe

It's said you keep the peace.
I study you for balance.
Will you never take my side? Even

as I duly write your essays –
Door as Keyhole Surgery,
Door as False Memory.

Did you know that
in the vestibule of door-makers
competition is unhinged?

Let's take a drive
to Doors R Us
and remind ourselves

that in our own lifetime
95% of doors
remain unopened.

Face up to it, Door.
Both ingrained,
we are not so different:

I have played the understudy
to the door
that played the understudy

to the iron railings
that played the understudy
to all the gates of hell.

I kiss the hinges of the door (just in case)

1.
a ritual
they hang
as fulcrum
to you and me

3.
if they are gold
I will flog them at market
a pocketful of hinges baked in a pie
I only saw them fall out once
Ottawa   Carlingwood Library
door hanging off one hinge
like a woman off a lamppost

6.
roving L-shape of hinge
for lover   learner
lascivious or lame
El L   toreador off-guard
who flaps his cape
a side-step to safety

14.
unhinged:
a wingless door

19.
plain contrariness
a cellist mid-flow
and in exile
the sadness that spat us out
before we knew

Relative Values – Me and Consciousness

***Me**, an artist in naïve ceramics, lives in a 1920s terrace and loves to play pontoon.*
***Consciousness**, controversially, has never had to survive on fixed wages. Their relationship can be described as off and on.*

Consciousness:

Me never got over the custody battle I had with Mind,
nor how it made headlines at the time.
I suggested a compensatory dog. Me named it Bishop,
not for godliness but for the diagonal moves.

It's true we're often at loggerheads, like being locked
inside a bathroom with no reason to come out.
I'll give context, leave teasers. I support
the projects Me has nurtured since childhood.

Yes, I enjoy skulduggery, and am perhaps
too tickled each time Me rages or rails.
Still, I watch, I love, attentive as a wasp
that noses sweet cups.

Me can see through this
and tries not to drink.

Me:

It's a tussle. The thing is, Consciousness
always steps it up after catching wind of me
then keeps me awake all night wondering
which of us is exempt from burning out.

Consciousness *can* be less inflammatory
and lie shtum, like a ball of wool in a white basket.
But if I try to level with Consciousness it's only
to inhabit more fully the mirage.

And what to do now Consciousness has found
the cubby-hole where I've hidden everything?
There's no escape. Wrench off a wedding ring
and the finger stays runnelled.

Consciousness is the in-joke
that swallows me whole.

Mes saints sans cafetières

Take it to the rankled streets.
Saints must forego cafetières
as a perk of their job.
Coffee stains the teeth
and I prefer saints with pearly whites
and their statues birdshit-free.
Though I've noticed saints with blots.
Perhaps it goes with the territory.
All those hurts.
And how else to earn their keep –
refusing to give up the monastery
the way the rest of us refuse to go in.
But a day imperilled by caffeine?
Vigils. *Espressos.*
Lauds. *Cappuccinos.*
Vespers. *Macchiatos.*
This cannot be.
I shall raise the cry
mes saints sans cafetières!
Saints must be deprived
or else I'm no more
than a mug at their feet.
Milk of the earth,
the serpent is coiling
and the word cankering the leaves
is *latte, latte, latte.*

Dough must not not enter the body

ii.

she bends
her head over
the toilet bowl

her white confessor

here she finds eloquence
and a receptive ear

Earthmonger

All your eggs addle in spring. The world
you crawl towards is looking for shelter.
Not the distractions: portrait of yourself
straddling a chasm. Or reading *A Hundred*
Plants to See Before ~~You~~ They Die. Bagging
one more bedevilled California condor,
red-brown eyes closed to the unweather.

But, my little ammonite (coiled and ancient),
my little armalite (sociopathic and sure):
we go back a long way, to one mating pair,
was it Lascaux, Genesis, or just vaguely
the Pleistocene – let them speculate.
Let them fashion from your rib a comely robot
who'll converse with you for ten whole minutes.

Earthmonger.
Everything slipping through your fingers.
See the bags being packed.
On its way out, the world smacks into you,
leaves a mess on your jacket,
the wing-smear
of something forever flying.

to know you are female does not help

your noise at the periphery
drumming up your relatives.

ah. already here. the touchy-feely mob.

I reach round his back and squash you one by one,
making oblations of the blood
each proboscis has sucked.

I'm in competition with you,
a borrowed bed, moonlight in slats
you zig across

you hussies
vixens
minxes
open-legged
            night-flyers.

morning
and his shoulders have erupted
in tiny coarse volcanoes,
dirty pricks of conscience.

A Voltage of Ghosts

Negative – Margaret's tea leaves dispensing futures

but not her own. The first dead person
I ever saw. Absurd absence: the body
on duty but Margaret gone AWOL.

Her heirloom teacups, porcelain,
imperilled, my thumbs too thumby.
Scratched blue Russian tea caddy,

lording emptiness. What draining away.
Ghost of tea, you burn my mouth
(the milk jug pouring its heart out).

Positive – 1989 again

Call in your own ghost.
Speak to your grandfather
on the night-shift.
To be haunted
is to be disenfranchised.
To be a spectre
is to be disenfranchised.
What kind of joke is it
in the dark of a bedroom
to be a throng of one.
A persecution of the living,
who react ungraciously.
But when the border gives way
the chancers will flood.
It'll be historic,
memorable, monumental.
You'll want a headliner,
wall-conquering as the Hoff.
A humdinger party. And Trabis
to arrive like the heavenly host.

god is my feeder my bearer of trays

his ease of movement among canned goods
not just canned goods but chocolate cake
not just the cake but loaves and fishes
and bagels, pretzels, four seasons pizza
the way that he and I collude
and not just collude but ham up our roles
me lauding him while he magnifies me
for god is my feeder my bearer of trays
and home delivery is all I demand
and doorstep deliverance is all I ask
and not just rescue but how in the night
when I wake up with designs on the moon
hogwild moon in the craving space
and my craving bursts through its seams
god is my feeder my bearer of trays
for him I aim to be fattest of all
for him I'll be airlifted then we'll elope
our future transcendent, our story immense:
he took this girl this malformed apple
the malformed apple expelled from the tree
the tree scribbled with roughcast prayers
the roughcast prayers perturbed by daylight
the daylight austere as a cedar plank
the cedar plank reformed as a chair
the chair intent on holding a shape
but hold a shape she would not do

The winter inside my mother

Winter was never nailed down, would slip
from my mother like an expletive that had
her reverting to forty below, trawling wastes
of blizzard-bent woods. Evenings, stretched
out on our sofa, she'd place her toes, lunatic
with cold, to burn in my lap. And I pictured her
in stinging drifts, hoar-scald on her face, nearly
a corpse yet scavenging berries for a child
growled to life in the gaping white.
                                        Always the Hibernian in her.
To worship snowfall. To cover her tracks.
And if I could say she ever found her way back
intact, it was only to bequeath the ice-melt stain
in the bureau drawer, with snapshot of her party trick –
to stand out on the road, join a line of leafless maples
and simply go bare.

snow is mutiny

long into the afternoon, you've wandered into snow that has the smell of linger, the sound of here, the most peaceful you can ever be, out in the vast vast, tracks erasing, the way back obliterated, the way forward expunged, you've stumbled on

the place to	lie still, the rebellion of snow over you, its tucks	numb cheekbones
while you	fold under the Betelgeuse star, you'll fall asleep	succumb to weight
and pressure	to warmth in your snowsuit, a soft micro-climate	you've craved as
anything that	gives birth on the sly, unlatches itself beyond you	takes on ever
more snow	where older siblings search, let them not discover	the forgotten
cipher to	how snow conjoins, never undresses or unsews	its private hoard
of cold	but ensures you'll be found centuries from now	preserved in
permafrost	*her mouth sucked mitts for minimal nourishment*	a short period
of time	all colour bleached from clothes gone stiff beneath	the drifts over
your shape	the flakes that heaped clemency, enshrined you	as if frost must
close in	up to the tiny nose-hole, the generosity of snow	to enchant
the bruises	to eke itself out, spread as far as the eye can hurt	while peripheral

hounds delay on the horizon before hunting in packs to unbury you from your sorry game, little pip dormant under the comforter, all idiom effaced, superfluous under the faultless sheet, leaving no clue, your sublime redaction, your blanket of absences

My best canvas

I've pegged it up
like the underlay of a crime scene
that proves a body blows its gasket
angry and punctual

I've smoothed it
into a square of drawn-thread work
to counteract sheepskin strips
once stuffed between the legs

I've hung it out
an oily rag that mopped excess
of everything that bore no fruit
a grafter's dirty protest

I've nailed it
as you would a winding cloth
whose selvedge of caramel and tea
is the signature of forgers

I've displayed it
as a contour map of ancient paths
and irrigation channels
the highest of all tides

I've dedicated it
to spillage and debris
this carcass
that left its animal behind

Up Yours, Wittenberg!

- How Luther became Reformation's poster boy
- In pictures: from innocent chorister to rapacious door-desecrator
- As soon as the coin in the coffer rings, the soul from purgatory springs

by our Disassociate Editor

You mentioned indulgences: take these. Robots and driverless cars and quick-sprints to the finish. Precision bombing. Rat-traps and travellators and laminated instructions. *The counter-tops must be kept clean*. And will be, because you never cook. Or eat, but are gaming upstairs – where your logging saw is no consolation. (The savannah-killer in you that'd have Clarence the Lion served up as a rug.) Meanwhile, I'll be the nail on that Wittenberg door, holding the effing document. Pinching the damn proclamation so tight it'll break out in hives. Driving hard, like driving into a wrist. Dancing on my points. Time for your 180-degree appraisal posted where everyone can see it. Lights on until the wee (corporate) hours, chary and ludicrous. It's Black Friday Saturday Sunday all over again and spiralling (student) debt, with tinpot dictators and tantrums when nothing's watchable on Netflix.

Let them eat worms.

Oh *pacem* painstaking Luther. Those theses.

Freewill says: it's all up to me.

Here I stand I can do no other.

She withholds her babies

one by one then
the twins then the triplets

She bunches them on a set of keys worn round her waist
busy chatelaine locking the vestibule

They trundle and race tricycles on the veranda
She trips up

She scribbles on their bloodline
nope and *nope* and *nope*

A teeny bat found half-alive in the grass
must go to the sanctuary

What is fecundity
if not loud and overbearing?

She thinks about this in the maternity wing where she makes tea
for the expectant too late to save

She will not bloat into mother
unlocking the unholy *desmadre*

No. Babies stack politely in the greenhouse
on the ledge of the people-carrier on the non-school run

She withholds babies
not to be engulfed

She withholds babies
not to set ice shelves cracking

She withholds babies until she can name them all
Absolom Abscissa Absentia…

her loose change of occasional finds
The babies are *here* (points to throat)

the babies are *here* (points to breastbone)
the babies are *here* (points to earlobe – hole where the stud once was)

Soulscammer

Something amiss. He rings mid-morning. Apparent malfunctions
deep in the machine. (Bony sockets unconnected, eyes fogging.
My mirror never runs dry.) He says he's KevinFromTechnicalSupport
who thinks I'm 'Mrs Gruff' of 'Tammies'. So be it, I'll play along,
yes, I've noticed flaws, misplaced icons. Workings gummed up.
All to be corrected, made spangly-new, sure, fix it, Kevin, I'll pay
whatever usury, whatever indulgence, a little mediaeval but let me
not be cut off, proscribed, my soul away on a boondoggle. The tricks

it gets up to! Once my soul hoicked itself above a petrol pump
with me barely attached – I gave chase, it nearly got clean away.
And once it took a scythe to my knees, a day of words in my ear,
he's dead, he's dead – no more chance… no more chance to…
My soul skived off in rivulets while I went ass about face,
cheap coffee from a cardboard cup rioting over flagstones.

Dough must not not enter the body

iii.

She holds her body to ransom.
Surely the negotiators will come.
It's in the balance.

Food is
life.
Food is
death.

How the body holds

its comforts and suggestions.
How it castigates and swelters.
Or hardens at night, tough as dirt.
How it holds intent like extent
and by that, how it holds hope,
spread like a mat.

How it thinks it is fixable.
Will lie on an operating table
and soak sheets with piss,
blood and fight.
Will take cure-alls,
and eat other creatures' organs.

How the body nurses grudges,
its intestines as trenches.
A long voyage.
Contortions and turns.
Food: it hits the mark.
Daily target practice.

How the body is a hero's circle
of infringements and hideaways.
A sublime store.
How it subsides under another's weight
only to crack and give up
its open-mouthed children.

How it holds daybreak
until it can no longer.

One out of every eight visitors attends the wrong hospital deathbed

Sublimating in blankets,
she is all-but-ghost

riding out the groan
of the mechanical mattress
in her backwater room,
the implausible language
I once woke up hearing.

Hard to twist it to lullaby,
bastardised Irish
I never got my tongue around,

or step in, practical
with *stay*
perhaps *go*
or *I'm sure your daughter didn't mean it.*

She seizes my index finger.
Never
has a digit been so adored.

I disengage,
take the spare folded sheet
from the bedside locker
and cut, with manicure scissors,
two holes for eyes.

I shall spook first.

My never-mother's skull
is a last-stand on the pillow.
A mouth of pointy teeth
glints, generous to the ploy.

Fiadh? she whispers.
Is it yourself?

Minus five minutes. Big Bang (sleeves rolled up) at the negotiating table

Come on Creationist, we're on
the same page. The *Word* you claim

will be the beginning is not unlike
my finger on the trigger. Granted

that this anteroom makes us nervy,
your mouth anticipating speech

is no better than a glottal stop.
You'll gag unless you breathe.

That's right. *In. Out.* And don't read
too much into my back-of-the-envelope

doodle which imagines you ice-bound,
cloven-hooved and with bifurcating antlers:

just a bit of fun. Look, there's barely
a matchstick between us. We've both tabled

our joint objective as speed. What's your seven days
set against my split-second to spawn

the whole enchilada? And I could downplay:
be a paltry Bang, a tongue-tied Bang,

a sidling-into-the-backrow-dripping-ice-cream-everywhere Bang,
a blink-and-you'll-miss-it Bang,

who'd still propel your garbling vowels,
plosives, fricatives, your coalescing song

ever outward, ever endward, where it will
finally be noted how you and I *gave it a go*.

How together we invented seeds
that blew their klaxon-flowers,

and unleashed such loudmouth stars
their verbosity blinded us.

Tambourine

The first I heard was when it rattled a roll-call
of lights to be switched off.
Then it flounced as parasol outside my back door,
battling a cantankerous July wind.

When it replaced the drum of my washing machine
and spun claggy clothes on eco-cycle
I saw how its underbelly could be flipped
and used to carry a tumbler of water

to the lectern/podium/pulpit for dry moments.
Of course I worried its presence signalled
a change of direction or loss of heart, and feared
it had zilch to say beyond its metallic zils

or worse, was just temping for the big-hitters,
buben, pandeiro and timbrel, until I saw Timsie
down the George and Dragon with a bicycle chain
round his neck, keeping time badly

to a tribute band's take on 'Tears of a Clown'.
One night a fox screamed. I woke to a bang
on my hip, the tambourine beating the life out of me.
I thought of St Teresa of Avila, her headaches,

and the museum in the Convent of San José
where two receptionists knitted and left me
in charge. No photos allowed, but I scribbled
an inventory of accoutrements required by a saint:

- saddle for journeys to religious houses
- handkerchief smirched with blood
- vacant sheet of parchment paper
- tambourine gussied with silver

The enemy is defeated by the sound of the tambourine.
Perhaps. But if painted in ochre on a Minoan vase,
I'd be the tambourine's temple dancer – enticing
a winged genie with ribbons and an almond branch.

Waterstabber

after 'Luncheon of the Boating Party' by Renoir

I'm not dog-broody.
Not for the cute
Affenpinscher
on Aline Charigot's lap,
future Mrs Renoir
with her pert nose.
Just want to deplete
bottles of red,
wear flirty *canotiers,*
potter the afternoon on
the far side of the river.
Sun-facing, a lavish profile.
Nice work, Pierre-Auguste,
pulling a scorcher –
men in white vests!
Had you but saved
some camembert,
the *tarte au citron.*
Had you but looked
past railings, thicketry,
and la-di-da sails
for my kayak,
hell-for-leather paddle.
J'arrive.
Showing my tricks.
Trying to tip and screw-roll
the boat – all misjudged
in pummel-currents,
hull up, head down.
Legs rammed
under the skin.
Blades lost.

My violent arms.
Lungs in damp pain.
J'arrive.
Pull me ashore
at the Maison Fournaise.
Let me eat grapes,
chat to Aline.
I know our rivers
have crossed.
Though mine is no Seine
but dyspeptic water.
Its mouth a disgrace.
All that spittle
never wiped away.

#PowerToPardonMyself 2

Numerous legal scholars
too numerous to mention
back me up.
Their sheer numerocity would astound you.
Apparently my pardon powers are supreme.

My lawyer attests to this in the letter
I made him write.
The person overseeing
any pardon of me
will be me.

I have the prerogative
as well as the genius and looks
to wipe the slate clean.
That's not to say I *will* pardon myself
or my associates or family.

I'm just exploring the reach
of my forgiveness.
Which I'm told is considerable.
Listen, I'm not going around stating
I can't wait to let myself of the hook.

Self-acquittal is not such a big deal.
And remember, when it comes to my record
there's no proven violation.
That doesn't mean I'll be lenient
if I need to hold myself to account.

I'll give due weight
to each of my arguments.
Many people say
you can't be the judge of your own case.
That a pardon is something

you can only give to someone else.
But when I belch and say *pardon me*
I'm taking responsibility for my own action.
It sounds like I'm involving you
but, believe me,

I'm not.

Dough must not not enter the body

iv.

Her belly is the barometer she touches each day.
It can be empty as a plundered well,
a ransacked house of bickering selves.

Or full as a basket of laundry.
A grain store for the unknown road.
Tight armour to fend off all blows.

Mostly her belly is a castle keep,
her face at the window
dishevelled.

'The light descends from nowhere'

– Wisława Szymborska

light knows winter needs help
and that I must get up
the most secret part of light
is a metronome
of inhale exhale
light's clothes are fibrous linen
my stinking retting
late-flowering
inane
light's eye burns harder
I'm always talking to you
sometimes
the light descends from nowhere
an afternoon with a coroner
whose words are kind

The tenants of faith

A hair's breadth from eviction

snitched by coffee mug rings on the chenille
putrid bins   not to mention
knuckleprints on the bedroom plaster

No dispensation for having rid the kitchen
of weevils

        the absentee landlord has me
        by the smallprint

Think: what luxury
even to be considered
faith's albeit deplorable tenant

I'm much more temporary
let's say a coldcaller on faith
pressing for a legible signature

or a doorstepper of faith
stalking its uproarious shindig

Faith should be
        forthcoming as hands
        cupping water

        pliant as my body was
        that winter morning
        under its wedding dress

Do not indulge indigo

even if it moons at your window   Do not feed indigo   as pit into which
you pour ledgers   or the branding on your arm   Do not romance indigo
unless you want stains never to go   Do not dig with indigo   your foot risks
limb-affecting disease   which is to say   your toes   will drop off
one by one   Do not carry indigo   like an organ donation card   you will be
winded   may as well shoplift   flat-packs from a self-assembly depot
or a pre-schooler   Do not exfoliate indigo   its flesh is spotted with liver marks
like your own   you a nascent witch   living in a hut   off the M3
Do not startle indigo   in its lair   while whelping   its young
are intransigent   but painting sub-Pollock pieces   Do not introduce indigo
into written phrases   it may fall short   as symbol of potency   or grief
Caveat emptor: do not deal in indigo   it will be cut with baking powder
e.g. The Great Indigo Crisis of 2017   Do not climb indigo   like a Munro
mobile phone signal dead   your face growing old in the wind
Do not map indigo   declare it a colony   where you offload petty criminals
and onload avocadoes   Do not sue indigo   it can rig juries   remember
the 'Hermanos Coloridos'   or pixelate indigo   as anything tentative
c.f. the theory of exits and entrances   Do not code indigo   in your conversations
no military circle   or listening post in the Pacific   will be fooled
Do not reduce indigo   to sloppy syllables *in dig go*   or get front-fixated
on no room at the 'in'   searching for shooting stars   Halley's Comet   Ursa Major
framed in the sky above your bed   or would be   if you didn't shiver
in the lock-up   with a corrugated iron roof   always leaking   and you thinking
in   indig   indignant   indigent   infradig   simply dug in

How to manifest anything you want – Storyboard 12

Scene 1: Close-up of an old-fashioned paternoster lift in a Paris hotel, let's say 8th arrondissement.

Imagine taking an elevator to the top of your head.

Scene 2: 19-year-old language student Mariana steps on the lift to get to your budget room under the eaves.

Think of continued ascent.

Scene 3: You answer her knock on the door. She says she slept out again last night and is convinced you're harbouring a supply of morning-after pills.

Banish unhappy thoughts.

Scene 4: You fumble purposefully in a drawer.

Focus on stepping out into an expanse.

Scene 5: Flash forward to Paris-Antibes afternoon train, arriving late,11.37 pm. Mariana prepares to sleep rough on the beach.

Manifesting
is the highest form of acceptance.

Scene 6: A pug-walking stranger convinces her she is taking risks in a public place and leads her to his apartment on Le Chemin des Âmes du Purgatoire.

N.B. Acceptance does not mean
mere tolerance.

Scene 7: He points to the sofa-bed that will be hers alone and asks if she is thirsty.

It's more an opening wide,
like a lemon tree
imparting all its fruit, pips, flesh.

Scene 8: She hears her father's last words, his lips parched: I'd give anything for some lemonade.

And you gather armfuls and armfuls.

Prayer workshop

We were all eyes to the front but aware
of our knees, smooth and untried.
We mouthed our afflictions, one by one, to strangers.
My neighbour took notes: material cadged for later.

Lunch, not provided, left room for grace
and radical intercessions, rain dances,
rosaries, spontaneous tongues.
Tibetan chanting toughened our lungs.

We hummed our way to night,
met in groups to trade devotions,
hyped them to pleas from the deathbed,
howls from the ravine, fell silent

as one man took from his shirt a prayer
shaped like a Zeppelin that lurched uncertainly
until, willed upwards only by our gaze,
it bobbed and nudged the rafters.

I once sat plum inside a ghost

Rather,
she overlapped me,

plumped my thoughts
as I shrank in hers.

I was pupil to her eyes,
addend to her sum.

I learned her name.
I learned her by heart.

She had me scrabbling bushes
to honour her grave.

The very same, I swear
could happen to you.

The tiniest change –
an umlaut cast over the air

or the twist of a guitar's peg. *Listen*:
with just one string tinned up

each chord's single jarring knot
is a flourish to jilt the ear.

Bit by bit perception unfields,
fresh inraids are made – your garden,

for instance: rain on every flare,
black cries on the grass,

the clouds of earth you turned,
the seasons you set stare by.

Easy. Fail on your knees.
Offer up your priors.

Usher in the die-light.
Believe the guests will come.

Dough must not not enter the body

v.

either
the body is tasteless
the body is gag
the body creases up

or
the body is tight
the body is skinflint
the body sits on its own blue hands

Our Lady of Deplorable Lapses

i. Daytrip

The town is at the end of all rivers and streams,
the border so close you can supervise entry and exit –
a straight line without rumours, in arresting light.

All of us are awake this spring season
when we look out of the window
towards the parish centre, arranged and clean.

For visitors: toilets and waste bins. And the statue
of Our Lady, made of polyester, 180 cm tall,
with crystal eyes, dominates the yard.

Pilgrims testify when you pray
how it changes the expression of the face
and the position of the hand.

They leave letters and decals with various desires,
then sit back in their buses or cars.
At the car park, passengers refresh themselves.

The area is famous for pain.
With no bridges
the dead could not be carried over the water.

Today the town has 1,200 believers
deployed in 360 families. But we have not seen
anyone anywhere: in the yard or on the road.

The parish is on extinction.
Many more people are dead than are born.
Those who are leaving have already gone.

There is no *curiously* on the windows.
In this town, like in heaven,
no women are married.

ii. The Come-Down

The statue was unbending and resolute.
The pilgrims saw its posture and stopped
dead in their tracks. More than homage –
it was the exact mirror of the statue.
Outside darkened. There came fractiousness
and little repose. Though *pose,* rather than
*re*pose, is everything to a statue.
Eternity may strike at any moment.
And the statue, steadfastly inanimate –
except to those versed in the Legend
of the Bountiful Wink – stood its ground.
Take it down. Off its pedestal, cried the pilgrims.
It too must stumble, stagger, acquire callouses.

And the statue acquiesced, at least
did not shake its head, wince, grimace,
or shrink back in affront. More pilgrims
gathered, a *plethora* of pilgrims
you could say, at the porch of the church,
in the chancel, the sacristy, the nave,
the choir stalls, swarming in devotional
fervour. They snapped group selfies
with the plaster figure who, though failing
to smile, or truly join in, registered
no displeasure even as it was prised,
manhandled and placed on a trundle-board.
And the pilgrims heaved and huffed

while sweat of beaten paths and byways
appeared under armpits of the good
and holy men – for it had been deemed
men's work to shift the sacred icon
that watched, not changing demeanour,
or preparing itself, save for the acceptance
of a robe of glittering almost-emeralds
wrapped around its shoulders. Fireworks
erupted as it travelled the streets, ambling
and shuffling, though it was the pilgrims
in truth who ambled, shuffled, and acquired
more callouses. Soon, feasting would commence,
for those who lugged and were weak
or empty of belly. And backslapping

would garland their efforts: that the statue
had been taken down a peg or two,
had come amongst them, had *trundled*.
Yet as they returned the prize to its place,
edging it through the Great West Door,
down the aisle – magnificent in its progress,
a biped Trojan horse – not even the Most Faithful
knew what might be hatching inside: whether
collywobble, foetus, cyst, or the wherewithal
to endure   endure

How old and sure the vapours are

The clouds are feral today.
Noting clouds on a clipboard is her task.
A pencil codes information, wet and floaty.

In adolescence she ate clouds. Snow in her throat, rain in her larynx.
A specious scudding –

never the clear sky of herself.
Little Fat Jacky Cloud
will steal your crackers, if allowed.

A cloudless sky has nothing/ everything to hide. Pristine, no mistake.
Do not bring your chaos.

She looks back in time. The almanac pose.
Clouds fly past, granular, historic.

They amass, do their thing, leave.
They lose their train of thought.

(Or form a ring above Alcázar de Venus, committing to the heavens,
saying, fall through here, this opening, to the earth. We will catch you.)

After which the sky rearranges itself, decorative.
On those days you cloudfully advanced,
she labelled herself terra mostly infirma,

held patchy ground in the giant-lapelled coat
you wrote a song about.

Together you carved windows with red frames, and a red gate.
Your walls rippled in humours of clouds.

You walked dusk
the aisle between day and night

while she stood at the doorway
in her bluster dress.

She is done with greyness.

To feed a sky on vapour
is as close as it comes to love.

That ye may be perfect and entire, wanting nothing

More ways to skin a cat, surely:
e.g. Wise Plover in her hovel

trafficking angel cards and runes.
There's too much trapped anger

she declared behind me, turning her palms
over my shoulders and lifting upward

as if I were a cantilever
collapsed on my very own frame.

I straightened, a tad. She offered
nothing more, save a cup of tepid

rooibos and the instruction
for calmness, to *think of the sea* –

which, of course, I saw everywhere, but abject
and scathing, its turmoil so spiked

by belligerent breakers that one day
I took the train to the coast,

resolved to finally settle matters.
I asked the sea to admit its failings.

It wouldn't leave the stones alone.

Rose window

Not in Sunday best, just as you are, you abseil
through the central boss of the rose window
saved miraculously from fire to deliver a sermon

on the perils of excess. The celebrant greets you:
he's going to lead us in prayer but you stammer
you aren't prepared for call or response, or even

to stay on script. No longer an impostor sweaty
in your own clothes from nights you haunted sleep,
coursing with darkness, careless of how it swilled you,

you admit lodestones, singular journeys, your hand close
in the front pew to mine. *Yes,* you say, *there's startling*
light when a roof has been blazed away. Charred arches

of stout timbers that soared and fell, gargoyles stacked
for safekeeping, a flying buttress bracketing the ruins –
all that stands defiant and what the elements will forgive.

The Platitudes

The last hurrah of the Bible, the book where all is laid flat, the placebo chapter which prettifies as duvet and hot water bottle rolled into one, the bedside-manner chapter that nods and scribbles its tropes into a folder, the deconstructionist chapter pestled to the lowest common denominator, and it is this: what you see is what you get, you finder-keeper, on your last legs of imagination while The Platitudes advance in their legions to scare you up to the *boudoir* (derived from the French, meaning *sulking room* – apt, n'est-ce pas?) because you can't read, much less dissect, much less parse the witless lines into syllabics or trills imitating the song of the hooded shrike, *tsr tzr krrrrrrr*, whose tart inflections carry the strain of each female carted off and incarcerated at that time of the month, for she waxes fey[1] and conniving unlike, perish the thought, old men gabbling in robes, sewn by women, their seams perfected before the advent of pinking shears, their edges scalloped, not ravelled.

---

1 The original Sumerian is decidedly equivocal. Translators have come to blows. Texts may vary. Texts *may* vary? Texts *do* vary.

Dough must not not enter the body

vi.

the shadow inflates
the body negates

the shadow defies
the body decries

the shadow unclenches
the body blenches

the shadow is blessed
the body suppressed

the shadow in sun
the body outdone

guardian angle

what if you sat the little girl down /
and said / stop these shenanigans / not landing a punch /
when your hair's yanked / ballsing up saltmustardvinegarpepper /
in the skipping rope / *scaredy cat* / *call that a jump* / *that leg*
is it yours / taut wire across bike racks / gravel in knee / so what
if it stings / just don't clam up / when the school nurse says /
scales and weights monstrous behind her / *you must tell your mother*
you eat too much
what if the little girl sat you down /
and said / don't panic / you can scrunch / into piddle-litter /
on the floor of a hutch / use femurs as whittling sticks / push yourself
back to the corner / into the angle / your guardian angle / if flipped
to a V / is a wingspan / to hold you / while the skirted skeleton /
cavorts past its mirrors / until just once in Lausanne / on Rue de Bourg
it will plague a shop window / and hear the glass say
enough

Baddendum

No amendment. Just the guts to say, this is how it ends.
Not a soft landing, but judders, bawling brakes. *That's all folks,*
the credits roll, roll, roll, six thousand names, and still you sit
in reupholstered cinema seats with a bucket of slobbery popcorn,
holding out for a fitting *finis* to *Ruminator 2, Procrastinator 4,*
whichever, you were invested in characters like the step-uncle
you never had, bringing puppies and pastilles. The killer's
just decamped in a dumpster car to Borneo to rustle up a bar
on the beach, for chrissake, no comeuppance, no takedown,
just credits of artistes you spit to thank, roll, roll, roll, yawn,
you rode out the whole three hours for a catch to be revealed,
while trapped (at worst) in *la salle* or (at best) in the foyer,
can I just get a coffee, no you cannot, begging the anointed
statue (donated by swindling loans company) to revive,
drop its loincloth, propose to you, as you wait for saints,
saviours, Santa – not your father or mine, but Real Santa,
feet up in Aspen, no snow*, suit unzipped, necking a beer.

*snow, as we know, is mutiny

Biography

She arrives headlong, moon in Capricorn.
And her name means
she who crosses oceans
(slipways and currents).
Wind in her father's hair.
A land too big
          to crayon on a page.

A clavicle is broken.
Thoroughbred Palomino
in a race in the woods,
she shied at a bough.

And her name means
she who allows the grass
to grow between her toes.
A split-afternoon high above Collioure.
Back of her legs squirmy
on the plastic seat of a stinking car.
Double her age, paunched, he lours.

Overnight, JFK, after a Dublin flight.
What godawful price
to have smiled at a man
in an irksome suit.
And her name means
she who pretends to dress up
and have everywhere to go.

She finds a map of ancestors crawling the grasses
          great-great-great-great grandmothers
drop babies on the ground
          coddle them close to the fire
as if the smell of meat has gone to their heads.

And she loves and is loved
and the millimetre separation of flesh
          from his
          the most daring of her gifts.
And she comes to him veiled.
Her veil is her wile.
She is short and closer to the dirt.
Her gown brushes the sphagnum moss.
Her shoes are pointed, just in case.

And a baby lurches inside her ribcage.
A kind of glee.

Like an earth tremor a daughter wakes her.
Like a thunderstorm a son shakes her.
Both children are stakes in her ground.

And her name means
she who has divided herself.

She spreads across him as ivy across a wall.
If she thieves light
it is only because of his complicit mortar.

Some days it is –
Him: levitation. Her: guy rope.
Other days it is –
Him: guy rope. Her: levitation.

Pond crossings river crossings sea crossings
the frozen expanses of DNA
replace her own hair with fur.
Daughter gone rogue.
          It's how she learned to skin
          and be skinned.

Night of the Long Writing
(for she condenses her life)
a computer spellchecks *précis*
adjusts for the accent on *précis.* ← it's done it again
Nothing can be left uncorrected.
She settles on the edges
part eyrie part bunker
part landfill part landfall

and cannot keep out of churchyards
brooding on headstones as if they are her own.
She wants to set something straight, other than bones.
And her name means
she who is the fly
prior to the flypaper.

Snow abandons Mulhacén.
Always a glitch about co-ordinates
and mileage
how precisely to get there.
Always a postulant in a ketch
who sails or capsizes.

Of course, the funerals.
She grieves vicarious
    on a tree by a river a little tom-tit
    cries widow not-widow not-widow.

The swagger of ash, air-ridden.
She sucks cinders into her lungs.
Whispers of body on her navy jacket.

How soon she too will evaporate
like dithering dew.
As she walks she loses it.
Even the caged wolf-whistling parrot
falls silent.

And her name means *she who has outrun.*

The garden is a jungle now.
Nothing wags, follows, or comes to heel.
Morning and night a noise, rough and canine,
rises in her throat.

And her name means
she who is beautiful veins
after the death of the leaf.

Dental records may refute the above.

S'Index

Additional notes on characters

I – central pillar of piece despite best efforts
to lie down. Single, but dating. Other characters
say domineering, notably **Me** – total punchbag
of **I** except in often-quoted email message
Me and Ptolemy went to the Jeff Koons Exhibition
showing confident assumption of subject role.
Despite temptation, tries not to fraternise with **You**
who, since English refuses to *tutoyer,* means *you,*
skulking on your own, as well as the whole
rickamatoot of *you* all in the shit together. **You**,
plotting to be both private and other or wave/waive
the singularity card. Motivation? Once got into
a department store elevator with Household Name
after **We** were caught checking out teal sofas with
throws – complicit, amorphous, yet hounded by
clingy and deteriorating **Body** who, if funding
unavailable, can be ditched altogether.

Notes

The Attitudes: in the Bible, *the Beatitudes* are eight blessings delivered during the Sermon on the Mount. Each phrase begins with the word 'blessed'.

Moonbather: excessive moonbathing can lead to moonstroke, otherwise known as 'night caress'. Hard to diagnose. Watch out for a face of instalments, a tongue of bitter chapters.

God's view of smoking was a headline on an edition of the Jehovah's Witness newspaper *The Watchtower* being given out free on a local street corner.

Mes saints sans cafetières is a sonic nod towards *médecins sans frontières.* Other titles in contention were:

Mes saints sans bétonnières	my saints without cement-mixers
Mes saints sans guêpières	my saints without corsets
Mes saints sans chatières	my saints without cat flaps

Nine sort-of truths and **Earthmonger** both appeared in *ORIGINAL PLUS DUB* (Hesterglock Press) where pairs of poets collaborated.

Earthmonger was originally entitled 'The Bond Street Reformulations' in response to Rishi Dastidar's poem 'The Bond Street revelations'. His contained the phrase *swinglungeburst* from which I coined *wingplungecursed,* the thematic starting point for my poem.

to know you are female does not help is part of Insect Love Songs, inspired by a workshop given by Fiona Benson. Her project with Arts and Culture at University of Exeter resulted in the anthology *In the Company of Insects.* www.youtube.com/watch?v=TxjXjYo-AjU

Up Yours, Wittenberg! *Here I stand, I can do no other* are words attributed to Martin Luther when he was summoned to the Diet of Worms in 1521 and subsequently denounced as a heretic by the Roman Catholic Church because of his opposition to the practice of payments to obtain papal indulgences, or forgiveness of sin. *As soon as the coin in the coffer rings, the soul from purgatory springs* is a couplet popularised by Dominican preacher Johann Tetzel.

Tambourine is after Jericho Brown's 'The Hammers' which was modelled on 'What the Angels Left' by Marie Howe. While St Teresa's blood-stained handkerchief and tambourine are certainly in the museum in the Convento de San José in Avila, Spain, one of her fingers is in the Convento de Santa Teresa in the same city, her left hand is in the church of Nuestra Señora de la Merced in Ronda, and her left arm and heart are in the Convento de la Asunción in Alba de Tormes.

'The light descends from nowhere' is from Wisława Szymborska's poem 'True Love'. The line *I'm always talking to you* comes from the Cat Stevens song 'How Can I Tell You' on the album *Teaser and the Firecat.*

Do not indulge indigo as second-prizewinner in the National Poetry Competition of 2018 had a film version commissioned by the Poetry Society and made by James Norton. vimeo.com/364013178

I once sat plum inside a ghost is a true story. Did you guess? More over a cup of coffee.

Our Lady of Deplorable Lapses *i Daytrip* is collaged from a Euro Line TS Tours and Travel Agency webpage, posted April 5 2018. Author: Kreso. I was charmed by the hiccups in translation. Many years ago, when cameras contained film, I took a picture of the statue, the Madonna of Tihaljina, famed for her extraordinarily lovely face. I wanted the snap to prove her beauty to others back home. No such luck. When the photo was developed, everything was there – except for the face.

That ye may be perfect and entire, wanting nothing is from the Bible, James 1:4, the King James Version. *But let patience have her perfect work, that ye may be perfect and entire, wanting nothing.*

guardian angle: some experts swear that guardian angles love ironmongery and will linger at the headboards of the overwrought.

Additional notes on characters: the word *ricmatic* is an Ullans (Scots-Irish) word meaning 'the whole lot'. My father's preferred variation was *rickamatoot,* which I have used here.

Acknowledgements

My thanks to the editors of *Finished Creatures, The Poetry Review, Primers: Volume One* and *ORIGINAL PLUS DUB*, and also to Arts and Culture at the University of Exeter, where versions of these poems first appeared.

A mega thank you to the powerhouse team at Nine Arches Press – to editor Jane Commane for her kindness, depth of perception, and belief in these poems, and to Angela Hicken for tireless and cheerful championing.

Endless cups of tea and countless thanks to Anna Steinberg for the sublime artistic vision she brought to the cover of this book.

My heartfelt thanks go to inspiring teachers who have helped me more than they can know: Moniza Alvi, Malika Booker, Helen Eastman, Anne-Marie Fyfe, Mimi Khalvati, Kathryn Maris, Pascale Petit, Myra Schneider, Henry Shukman, Catherine Smith, Stephen Smith. Not just to poetry teachers, but those with wise and timely words – Julie Urquhart and Elizabeth Cappetta – and one who has been a magic mentor over many years: Meg Robinson.

I'm also profoundly grateful for advice and enthusiasm from poetry colleagues: Jill Abram, Fahad Al-Amoudi, Charlotte Ansell, Dean Atta, Vicky Bell, Keith Bossard, Hanne Busck-Nielson, Geraldine Clarkson, Courtney Conrad, Anne Enith Cooper, Tom Cunliffe, Rishi Dastidar, Mary Earnshaw, Beatriz Echeverri, Hannah Gordon, Chris Hardy, Elizabeth Horsley, Mehmet Izbudak, Seraphima Kennedy, Maisie Lawrence, Arji Manuelpillai, Be Manzini, Mary Mulholland, Kareem Parkins-Brown, Soul Patel, Matthew Paul, Michelle Penn, Janett Plummer, Peter Raynard, Bernadette Reed, Gillie Robic, Dorothea Smartt, Pat Smith, Joolz Sparkes, Kostya Tsolakis, Jill Watson and Naomi Woddis.

I am blessed to have a cocoon of support from my mother, and my siblings and their children. In particular I'm indebted to my closest family – Cris, Anne and Will – for unfailing understanding and love, and for putting up with, well, everything.

Everlasting gratitude to Stuart White, David Griffiths and Kathleen Robb.